LEARN TO PLA...

C000166126

ELECTRONIC KEYBOARD

by
Gary Turner

Published by
KOALA MUSIC ™
PUBLICATIONS

10 EASY LESSONS LEARN TO PLAY ELECTRONIC KEYBOARD
I.S.B.N. 978 1 86469 109 2
Order Code: CP-69109
Acknowledgments
Cover Photograph: Phil Martin
Photographs: Phil Martin

For more information on this series contact;
LTP Publishing Pty Ltd
email: info@learntoplaymusic.com
or visit our website;
www.learntoplaymusic.com

Contents

Introduction

10 EASY Lessons for ELECTRONIC KEYBOARD assumes you have no prior knowledge of music or playing the KEYBOARD.

This book will show you:
1. How to play over 25 songs using a range of two octaves.
2. Major, Minor and Seventh chords.
3. 12 Bar Blues and Turnaround progressions.

The book also features a chord chart section featuring over 50 different chords. The best and fastest way to learn is to use this book in conjunction with:
1. Buying sheet music and song books of your favourite recording artists and learning to play their songs.
2. Practicing and playing with other musicians. You will be surprised how good a basic keyboards /drums/bass/guitar combination can sound even when playing easy music.
3. Learning by listening to your favourite CD's.

All keyboard players should know all of the information contained in this book.
After completing this book you will have a solid understanding of basic keyboard playing and will be ready for further study on specific styles of music.

Approach to Practice

From the beginning you should set yourself a goal. Many people learn keyboards because of a desire to play like their favourite artist (e.g. Elton John), or to play a certain style of music (e.g.Rock, Blues etc.). Motivations such as these will help you to persevere through the more difficult sections of work. As your playing develops it will be important to adjust and update your goals.

It is important to have a correct approach to practice. You will benefit more from several short practices (e.g. 15-30 minutes per day) than one or two long sessions per week. This is especially so in the early stages, because of the basic nature of the material being studied. In a practice session you should divide your time evenly between the study of new material and the revision of past work. It is a common mistake for semi-advanced students to practice only the pieces they can already play well. Although this is more enjoyable, it is not a very satisfactory method of practice. You should also try to correct mistakes and experiment with new ideas.
It is the author's belief that the guidance of an experienced teacher will be an invaluable aid in your progress.

Using the Recording

It is recommended that you have a copy of the accompanying recording that includes all the examples in this book. The book shows you where to put your fingers and what technique to use and the recording lets your hear exactly how each song should sound. Practice the song slowly at first, gradually increasing tempo. Once you are confident you can play the song without stopping the beat, try playing along with the recording. You will hear a drum beat at the beginning of each song to lead you in and help you keep time.

A small diagram of a compact disc with a number as shown indicates a recorded example.

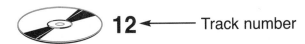 **12** ⟵——— Track number

Parts of the Keyboard

Although there are many different makes of keyboard available, they all have the following features in common:

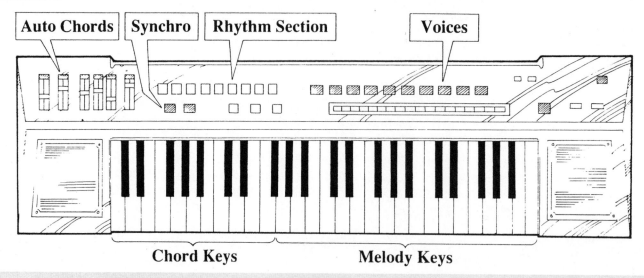

Voices

Keyboards offer a wide variety of instrument sounds. The instrument sound you choose is called a **voice.** Before you play a song, choose a voice that you like. Practice selecting different voices, and remember the settings for the ones you prefer. Look at your keyboard owners manual to help you. When you play the songs in this book, you can use any sound you wish. For some songs, you may wish to have a violin sound, for others you may prefer a trumpet, or a combination of several instruments.

Rhythm Section

The rhythm controls provide drumbeats to play along with. These drum rhythms can be changed to suit the kind of song you are playing. For example, in some songs you may want a Rock rhythm, in others you may want a waltz or a samba. Practice selecting different rhythms.

Auto Chords

These controls provide easy chords and bass notes to play along with the melody.

Synchro

This control allows you to stop and start the drums, bass and chords.

Melody Keys

The melody keys are used to play the tune of the song. Use your **right** hand.

Chord Keys

The chord keys are used to play along with the melody. They make the song sound full. Use your **left** hand.

Other Functions

There are many different brands and models of keyboards available, each having its own special functions. Ask your teacher or consult your owners manual for help in using these features.

Music Notes

There are only **seven letter names** used for notes in music. They are:

A B C D E F G

These notes are known as the **musical alphabet**. They are the names of the **white keys** on the keyboard.

The Keyboard

The black keys always appear in groups of **two** or **three.** The **C** note is a white key. It is always on the **left** hand side of a group of two black keys.

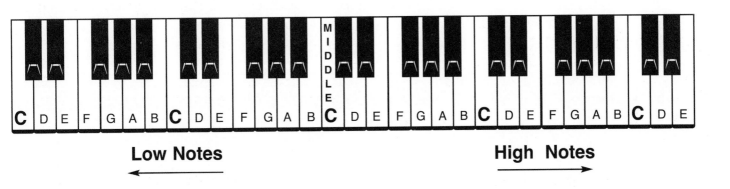

Low Notes
←

High Notes
→

How to Find Middle C

The first note you will learn to play is **Middle C**. Middle C is the note in the middle of the piano keyboard. This is usually the **third** C note from the left hand side. On some smaller keyboards, Middle C is the second C note from the left. If you are not sure, listen to the Middle C note in example 1 on the recording (see page 7). Play Middle C with your **right hand thumb**.

Fingers

The left and right hand fingers are numbered as shown below.

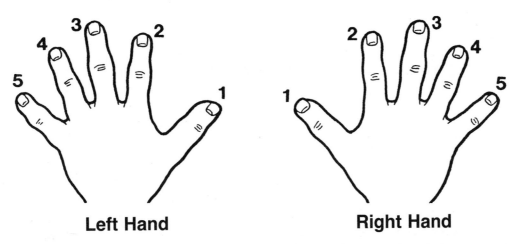

Left Hand   **Right Hand**

The thumb of each hand is counted as the **first** finger and has the number **1**.

Lesson 1

How to Read Music

Fourth space →
Third space →
Second space →
First space →

← Fifth line
← Fourth line
← Third line
← Second line
← First line

These five lines are called the **staff** or **stave**.
Music notes are written in the spaces and on the lines of the staff.

Treble Clef

This symbol is called a **treble clef**. There is a treble clef at the beginning of every line of keyboard music.

Treble Staff

A staff with a treble clef written on it is called a **treble staff**. Notes on the treble staff are usually played with your **right** hand.

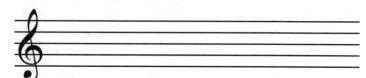

Music Notes

There are only seven letters used for notes in music.

A B C D E F G

These notes are known as the **musical alphabet**.
Keyboard music is commonly written in the spaces and on the lines of the treble staff. In this book the letter name of each note is placed inside the note head.

Note and Rest Values

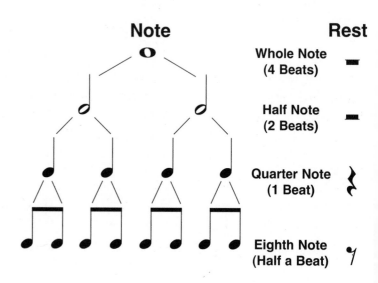

	Note		Rest
	○	Whole Note (4 Beats)	▬
	♩	Half Note (2 Beats)	▬
	♩	Quarter Note (1 Beat)	𝄽
	♫	Eighth Note (Half a Beat)	𝄾

The Quarter Note

← stem

← note head

This musical note is called a **quarter note**.
A quarter note lasts for **one beat**.

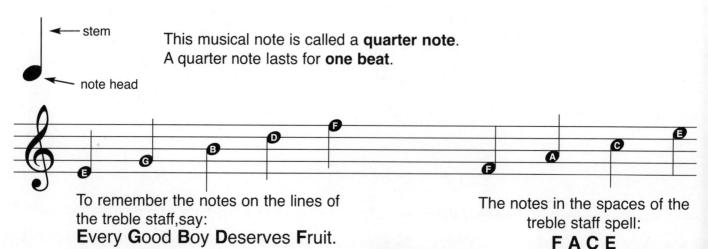

To remember the notes on the lines of the treble staff, say:
Every **G**ood **B**oy **D**eserves **F**ruit.

The notes in the spaces of the treble staff spell:
F A C E

Music is divided into **bars** (sometimes called **measures**) by **bar lines**. In this example there are two bars of music.

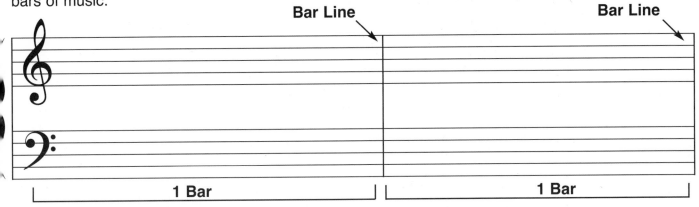

Bar Line   **Bar Line**

| 1 Bar | 1 Bar |

The Four Four Time Signature (4/4)

The two numbers after the clefs are called the **time signature**.

This is called the **four four** time signature. It tells you there are **four** beats in each bar. There are **four** quarter notes in one bar of 4/4 time.

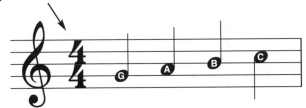

The Notes Middle C, D and E

Middle C is written just below the treble staff on a short line called a **leger line**. See page 5 to locate middle C on the keyboard.
• Middle **C** is played with the **first** finger (thumb) of your right hand.
• The **D** note is played with the **second** finger of your right hand.
• The **E** note is played with the **third** finger of your right hand.

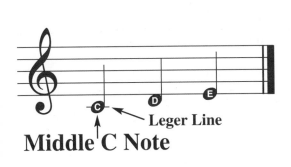

Leger Line

Middle C Note

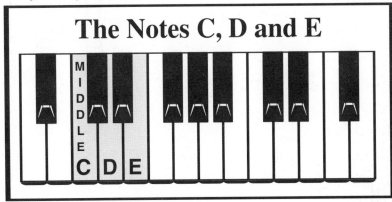

1.

In the following example there are four bars of music, two bars of middle **C** (bars 1 and 4), one bar of the **D** note (bar 2) and one bar of the **E** note (bar 3). There are four quarter notes in each bar.

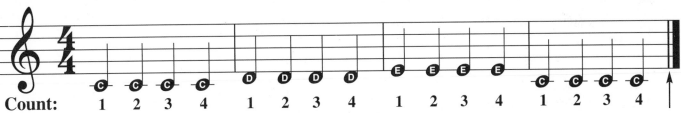

Count: 1 2 3 4   1 2 3 4   1 2 3 4   1 2 3 4

The **double bar** at the end indicates that the example has finished.

The Half Note

This is a **half note**. It lasts for **two** beats. There are **two** half notes in one bar of $\frac{4}{4}$ time.

Count: **1** 2

The Whole Note

This is a **whole** note. It lasts for **four** beats. There is **one** whole note in one bar of $\frac{4}{4}$ time.

Count: **1** 2 3 4

The **larger bold** numbers in the count indicate that a note is to be played. The **smaller** numbers indicate that a note is to be held until the next bold number (note).

 ## 2. In the Light of the Moon

Suggested Voice : PIANO

This song contains **quarter**, **half** and **whole** notes. Make sure you use the correct finger for each note and follow the count carefully.

These two dots are a **repeat sign** and indicate that the song is to be played again.

Count: 1 2 3 4 1 2 3 4 1 2 3 4 1 2 3 4

The Notes F and G

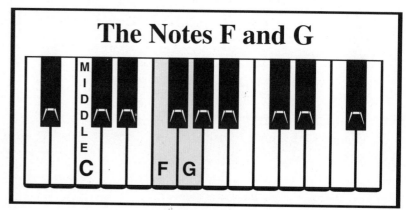

The Notes F and G

- The **F** note is played with the **fourth** finger of your right hand.
- The **G** note is played with the **fifth** finger of your right hand.

 ## 3. Aura Lee

Suggested Voice : PIANO

The song Aura Lee contains 8 bars of music in $\frac{4}{4}$ time. Remember to count as you play to help you keep time.

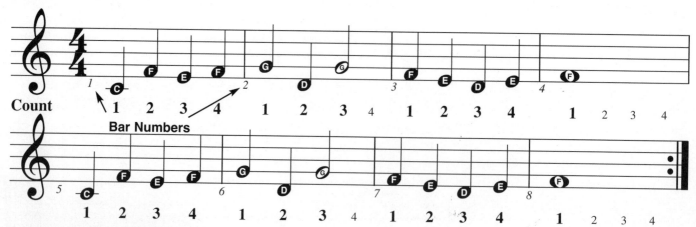

Count 1 2 3 4 1 2 3 4 1 2 3 4 1 2 3 4

Bar Numbers

1 2 3 4 1 2 3 4 1 2 3 4 1 2 3 4

Things to Remember
1. Play the keys with the **tips** of your fingers.
2. Keep your fingers **curved**.

Lesson 2

Chords

A **chord** is a group of notes which are played together. Chords are used to play along with the melody of a song. On electronic keyboards, it is possible to play a chord using only one finger. Find the **auto bass chord section** (eg Yamaha keyboards), or **Casio-chord section** (eg Casio keyboards),or **chord intelligence** (eg Roland or Kawai keyboards) and select the **single finger** position, or **on** position. This will allow you to play chords using only one or two fingers. On a piano, chords are played with three, four or sometimes more fingers. Chords are usually played with the left hand and the melody is played with the right. The first chord you will learn is **C major**, usually just called the **C** chord.

The C Major Chord

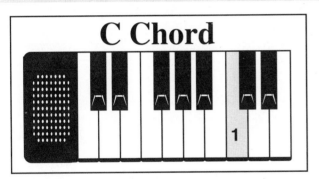

Chord Symbol

C

To play the **C** chord, touch the **C** key (as shown on the diagram) with the **thumb** of your **left** hand.

Any major chord can be played in this manner by simply pressing the key which has the **same letter name** as the chord.

Seventh Chords

Another common type of chord is the **Dominant seventh** chord, usually called a **seventh** chord. A seventh chord is indicated by the number **7** written after the chord name, eg: the G seventh chord is written **G7**.

The fingering you use to play a seventh chord will depend on which brand of keyboard you own. In this book we give the three most common fingerings, **Type 1** fingering, eg: **Yamaha** keyboards, **Type 2** fingering, eg: **Casio** keyboards, and **Type 3** fingering, eg: **Roland** and **Kawai** keyboards. If you have another brand of keyboard, check in your owners manual to see which fingering should be used.

Type 1 keyboards (eg: Yamaha and Technics) To play a seventh chord on this type of keyboard, press the **chord key** together with any **white** key to its left. Any seventh chord can be played this way.

Type 2 keyboards (eg: Casio) To play a seventh chord on this type of keyboard, press the **chord key** together with **any two** keys to its right. Any seventh chord can be played this way.

Type 3 keyboards (eg: Roland and Kawai) To play a seventh chord on this type of keyboard, press the **chord key** together with the **second** key to its left. Any seventh chord can be played this way.

The G Seventh Chord

Chord Symbol

G^7

Type 1 Keyboards
(eg: Yamaha and Technics)

To play a **G7** chord on this type of keyboard, press the **lowest G** key with the **fourth** finger of your left hand, together with the **white** key immediately to its **left,** using your **fifth** finger.

Type 2 Keyboards
(Casio)

To play a **G7** chord on this type of keyboard, press the **lowest G** key with the **fourth** finger of your left hand, together with the **two white keys** to its **right,** using your **third** and **second** fingers.

Type 3 Keyboards
(eg: Roland and Kawai)

To play a **G7** chord on this type of keyboard, press the **lowest G** key with the **fourth** finger of your left hand, together with the **second key** to its **left,** using your **fifth** finger.

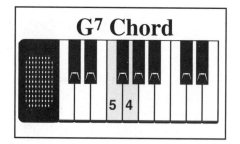

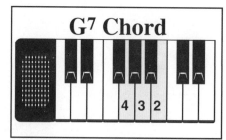

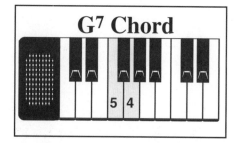

Using the Rhythm Section

When you add chords to a song, the keyboard also allows you to have a bass and drum accompaniment at the same time. Chords are indicated by **chord symbols**, which are written above the staff. In example 4 there are two bars of the **C** chord followed by two bars of the **G7** chord. To play example 4:

1. Set up the one-finger chord function on your keyboard.
2. Select a **rock, disco,** or **march** beat from the rhythm section.
3. Find the switch called **synchro/start** (eg: Yamaha keyboards), or **synchro** (eg: Casio, Technics, Roland and Kawai) and press it.
4. Press the **C** chord key and release it immediately. Your keyboard will begin playing a **C** chord with bass and drum accompaniment, and continue playing until you press another key, or the stop button. Look in your owners manual if you need more help to use this feature.

Next to example 4 there is a suggested rhythm to use. You can, however, use any voice or rhythm you like.

 4.

Suggested Rhythm: ROCK

Press the **C** key **once** and let the chord play for two bars, then press the **G7** keys and let the G7 chord play for two bars. Repeat this exercise, as indicated by the repeat dots, then press the **stop** button. Once you have pressed a chord key, the chord will continue to play automatically, so you will have time to move your fingers into a new position for the next chord, if necessary.

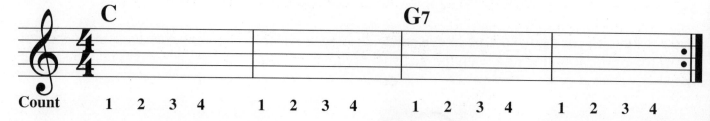

Songs With Chords

Before playing songs with chords, practice each part separately. First practice the **melody** of the song by itself (**right hand part**), then practice the **chords** by themselves (**left hand part**). Once you have learnt both parts, play them together. Before you play, adjust the tempo to a comfortable speed. To do this, press the **start** button, and the drums will play by themselves. If the drums are too fast, slow the speed down by adjusting the **tempo** control. You can increase the speed as you become more confident playing the song. If you are playing along with the recording, play only the right hand part. In this book, a chord symbol is only written above a bar when it is necessary for you to press a key or change chords. Eg: in example 5, just play the **G7** chord once at the start of bar **2**, and let the keyboard play for two bars.

Endings

Most electronic keyboards have a control which can automatically add an ending to songs you are playing. Press the **ending** button when you have finished playing a song. The ending feature has been used in most of the examples on the recording. Next to each example and song there is a suggested voice and rhythm to use. You can, however, use any voice or rhythm that you think suits the song.

| Suggested Voice : FLUTE |
| Suggested Rhythm: ROCK |

 5.

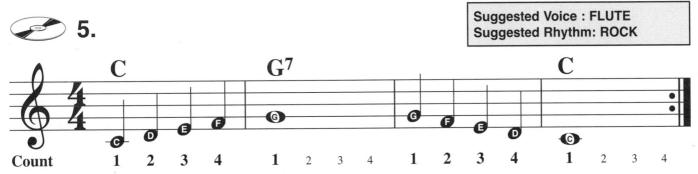

Remember to take your finger off the chord key immediately after you have played it, but keep your left hand fingers close to the keyboard, ready to play the next chord. Practice slowly and evenly, and count as you play. The chords are called the **accompaniment.**

| Suggested Voice : TRUMPET |
| Suggested Rhythm: SLOW ROCK |

6. Ode to Joy   **Ludwig van Beethoven**

This song is the melody to **Beethoven's 9th Symphony**. It contains **two** chords in bar 8, where each chord receives two counts.

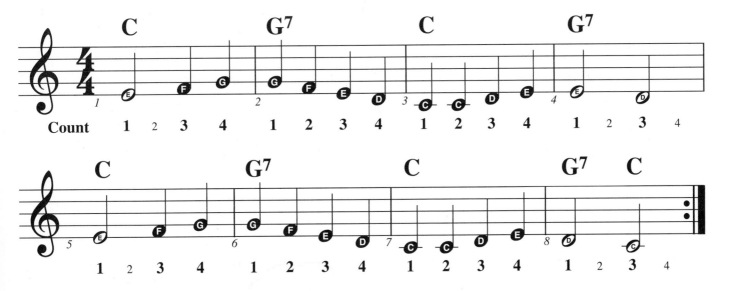

The Quarter Rest

Lesson 3

 This symbol is a **quarter rest**. It means **one beat** of silence. Do not play any note. Remember that small counting numbers are placed under rests.

Count: 1

Count: 1

 ## 7. Good Evening Friends

Suggested Voice : SAXOPHONE

There is a quarter rest on the first beat of the first bar.

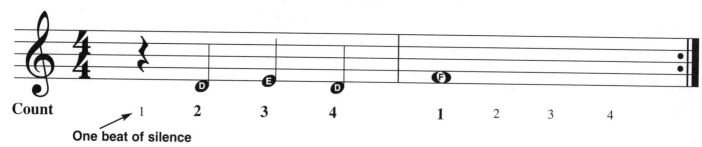

Count 1 2 3 4 1 2 3 4

One beat of silence

The F Chord

To play the **F** chord, touch the **lowest** F key.

Play the **F** chord with the **fifth** finger of your left hand.

Chord Symbol

F

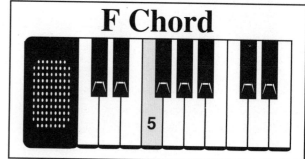

The Half Rest

This is a **half rest**.
It indicates **2 beats** of silence.

Count: 1 2

 ## 8. The Banks of the Ohio

Suggested Voice : ELECTRIC PIANO
Suggested Rhythm: COUNTRY

Sometimes you will see the letters **N.C.** written above music. This means **no chord**, so you cannot play any chord until a chord symbol appears.

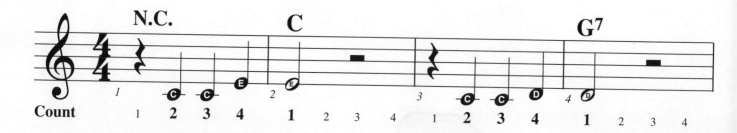

Count 1 2 3 4 1 2 3 4 1 2 3 4 1 2 3 4

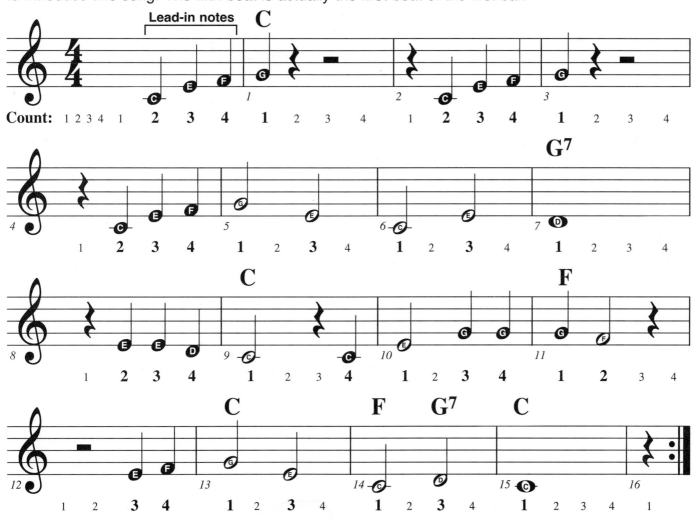

The Lead-in

Sometimes a song does not begin on the first beat of a bar. Any notes which come before the first full bar are called **lead-in notes** (or **pick-up notes**). When lead-in notes are used, the last bar is also incomplete. The notes in the first and last bar add up to one full bar. When playing songs with a lead-in, do not press the chord key until the first beat of the first full bar.

 9. When the Saints Go Marchin' In

| Suggested Voice : TRUMPET |
| Suggested Rhythm: DIXIELAND |

When the Saints Go Marchin' In is an early Jazz standard made popular by brass bands in New Orleans.The song contains both quarter and half rests. On the recording there are **five** drumbeats to introduce this song. The fifth beat is actually the first beat of the first bar.

Lesson 4

The Three Four Time Signature

3/4 This time signature is called the **three four time signature**. It tells you there are three beats in each bar. Three four time is also known as waltz time. There are **three** quarter notes in one bar of 3/4 time.

The Dotted Half Note

A **dot** written after a note extends its value by **half.**
A dot after a half note means that you hold it for **three** beats.
One dotted half note makes one bar of music in 3/4 time.

Count: 1 2 3

10. Austrian Waltz

Suggested Voice : VIOLIN
Suggested Rhythm: WALTZ

This song is in 3/4 **time** and contains dotted half notes. On the CD there are six beats introduction to this song.

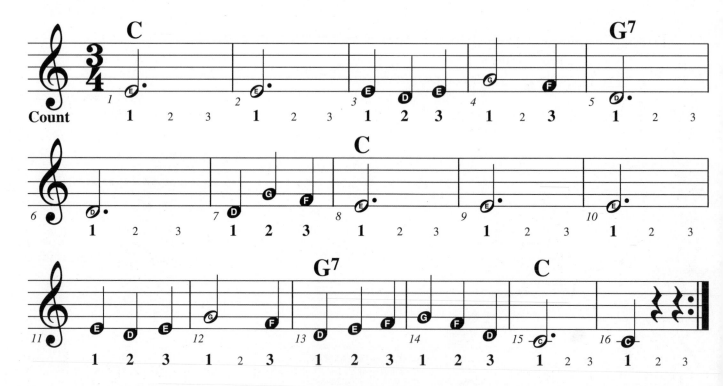

Legato

The next song contains two curved lines called **slurs.** A slur indicates that the notes written above (or sometimes below) it, should be played **legato.** Legato means to play the notes smoothly, so that they sound connected to each other. To play notes legato, keep your finger on the key until you have started to play the next key.

11. Orange Blossom

This song contains dotted half notes and is played **legato**.

Suggested Voice : CELLO
Suggested Rhythm: WALTZ

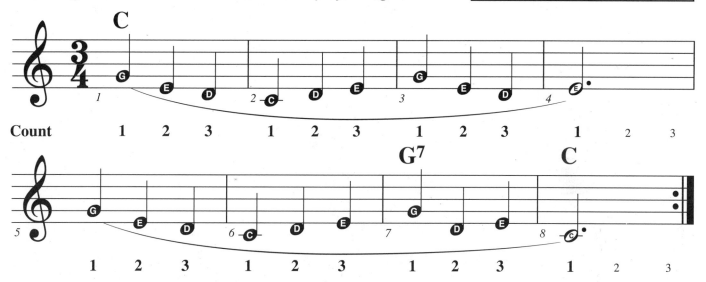

Staccato

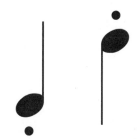 A **dot** placed above or below a note tells you to play it **staccato**. Staccato means to play a note short and separate from the other notes. To play a note short, lift your finger off the keys as quickly as possible.

 ## 12. The Mexican Hat Dance

This song has a lead in in ¾ time and uses staccato notes. On the recording there are **five** drumbeats to introduce this song.

Suggested Voice : CLARINET
Suggested Rhythm: WALTZ

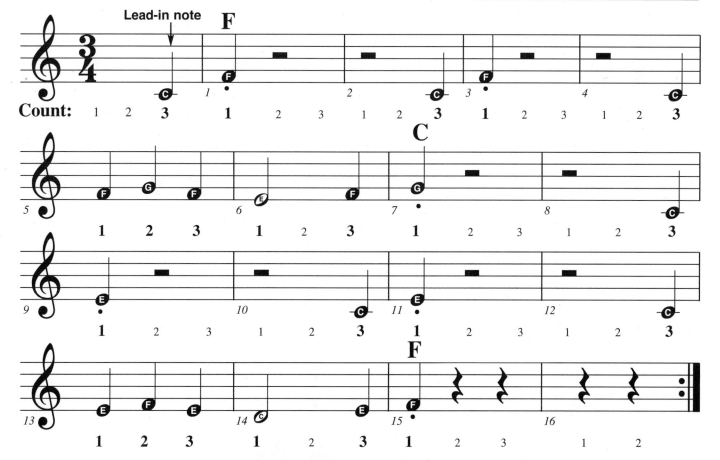

Lesson 5

The Notes A, B and C

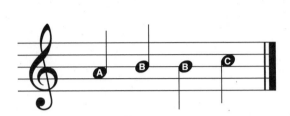

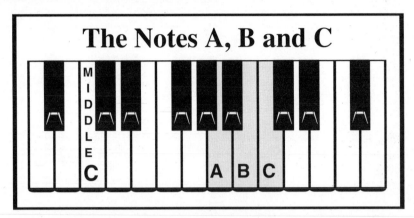

Notes written above the middle line of a staff usually have their stems going **down.** Notes written below the middle line of the staff usually have their stems going **up.** The stem for the **B** note can go **up or down**.

The C Major Scale

A **major scale** is a group of eight notes that gives the familiar sound:

Do Re Mi Fa So La Ti Do

You now know enough notes to play the **C major scale**. To play the C major scale smoothly you will need to play the **F** note with your thumb. Do this by moving your thumb **underneath** your second and third fingers on the way **up** the scale. On the way **down** the scale, move your second and third fingers **over** your thumb. This is called the **crossover**.

The small numbers placed above or below notes on the staves tell you which finger to play the note with. Be sure to use the correct finger.

13.

Suggested Voice : PIANO

The Octave

An **octave** is the range of eight notes of a major scale. The **first** note and the **last** note of a major scale always have the same name. In the C major scale, the distance from **Middle C** to the **C** note above it (or below it) is one octave (eight notes). All the songs you have studied so far, and the next song use notes from the Cmajor scale. Pay close attention to any fingering numbers above the notes. It is important to use the indicated fingering, as this will make the songs easier to play. Use this same fingering every time you play the songs.

The Tie

A **tie** is a curved line that connects two notes with the **same** position on the staff. A tie tells you to play the **first** note only, and to hold it for the length of both notes.

 14.

Play the **C** note and and hold it for six beats.

Suggested Voice : PIANO

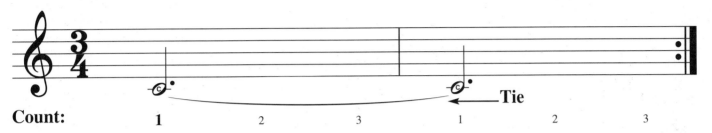

15. La Spagnola

Suggested Voice : ACCORDION
Suggested Rhythm: WALTZ

La Spagnola uses notes from the **C major scale** and uses the **thumb under** between bars 20 and 21. Do not confuse the tie with the legato slur which was introduced on page 14.

The Eighth Note

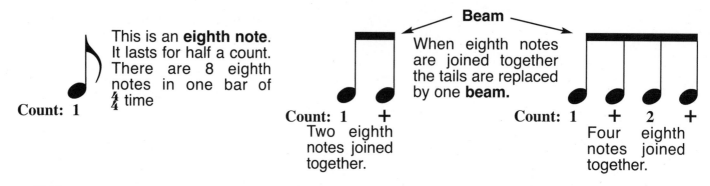

This is an **eighth note**. It lasts for half a count. There are 8 eighth notes in one bar of $\frac{4}{4}$ time

Count: 1

Beam

When eighth notes are joined together the tails are replaced by one **beam**.

Count: 1 +
Two eighth notes joined together.

Count: 1 + 2 +
Four eighth notes joined together.

 ## 16. How to Count Eighth Notes

Suggested Voice : PIANO

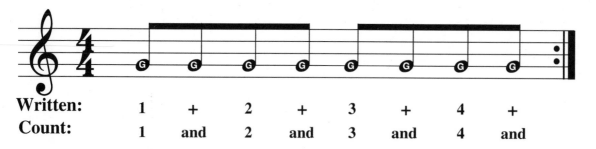

Written: 1   +   2   +   3   +   4   +
Count: 1   and 2   and 3   and 4   and

 ## 17. Shave and a Haircut

Suggested Voice : PIANO

There are two eighth notes on the second beat of the first bar. The notes in the second bar are played staccato.

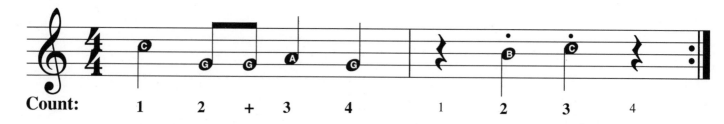

Count: 1   2   +   3   4   1   2   3   4

 ## 18. Rock Riff 1

Suggested Voice : SAXOPHONE
Suggested Rhythm: ROCK

On the recording there is a **one bar** introduction played at the beginning of this example. If your keyboard has an **intro** button, practice using it before each example.

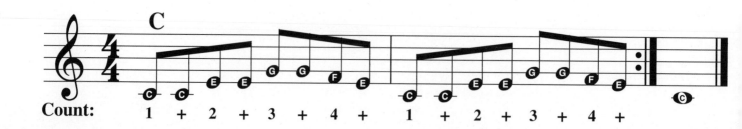

Count: 1   +   2   +   3   +   4   +   1   +   2   +   3   +   4   +

Key of C Major

When a song consists of notes from a particular scale, it is said to be written in the **key** which has the same name as that scale. For example, if a song contains notes from the **C major scale**, it is said to be in the **key of C major**. Nearly all the songs you have studied so far have been in the key of **C major**.

Suggested Voice : FLUTE
Suggested Rhythm: WALTZ

 19. Lavender's Blue

Suggested Voice : BANJO
Suggested Rhythm: COUNTRY

20. Pick a Bale of Cotton

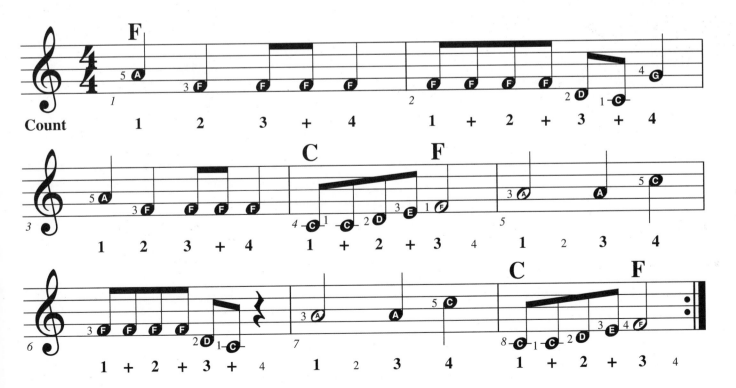

Lesson 6

The G Chord

To play the **G** chord, touch the **lowest G key** (as shown on the diagram) with the **fourth** finger of your left hand.

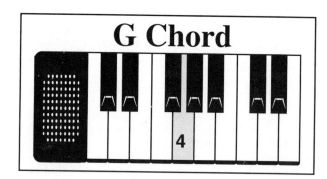

The D Seventh Chord

Type 1 Keyboards
(eg: Yamaha and Technics)
To play a **D7** chord on this type of keyboard, press the **lowest D** key with the **thumb** of your left hand, together with the **white** key immediately to its **left,** using your **second** finger.

Type 2 Keyboards
(Casio)
To play a **D7** chord on this type of keyboard, press the **lowest D** key with the **third** finger of your left hand, together with the **two white keys** to its **right,** using your **second** finger and **thumb.**

Type 3 Keyboards
(eg: Roland and Kawai)
To play a **D7** chord on this type of keyboard, press the **lowest D** key with the **thumb** of your left hand, together with the **second key** to its **left,** using your **second** finger.

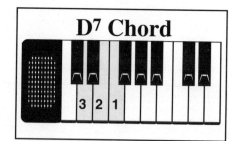

21. Hush Little Baby

Suggested Voice : GLOCKENSPIEL
Suggested Rhythm: BOSSA NOVA

This popular children's song makes use of the chords **G** and **D7**.

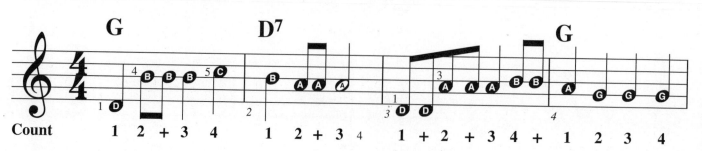

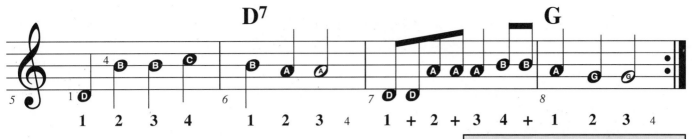

 22. Tom Dooley

Suggested Voice : GUITAR
Suggested Rhythm: COUNTRY

On the recording there is a **four bar** introduction to this song. When playing the melody, be careful to play the correct timing in bars **9**, **11**, **13** and **15**. Practice the timing in these bars separately before playing the complete song.

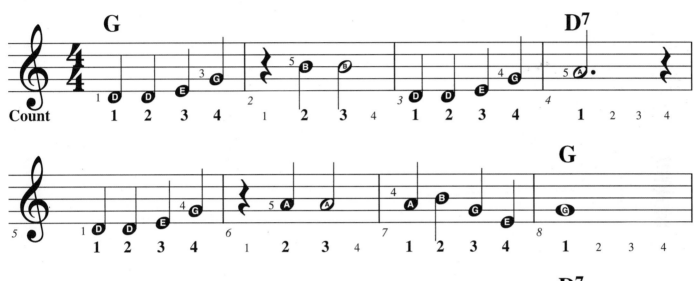

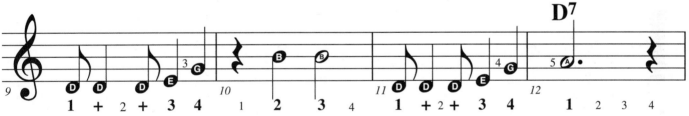

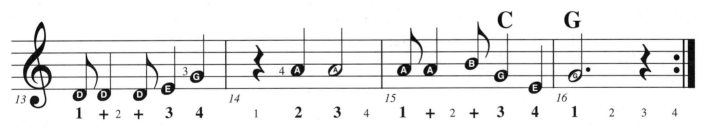

Another Note D

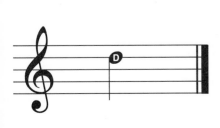

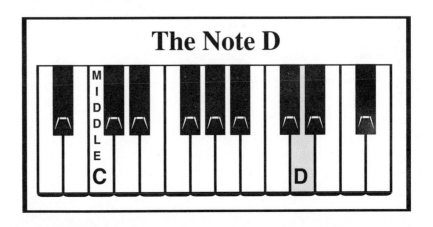

The Triplet

Count: **1** **+** **a**
Say: **one** **and** **ah**

A **triplet** is a group of **three** evenly spaced notes played within **1 beat**. Eighth note triplets are indicated by three eighth notes grouped together by a bracket or a curved line and the number **3** written either above or below the group. The eighth note triplets are played with a third of a beat each. **Accent** (play louder) the first note of each triplet group as it will help you keep time.

 ### 23. Amazing Grace

Suggested Voice : ORGAN
Suggested Rhythm: WALTZ

Amazing Grace is a gospel song which contains eighth note triplets, and also uses the new **D** note introduced on the previous page.

Sharp Signs

 This is a **sharp** sign.

When a sharp sign is placed before a note on the staff, it indicates that you play the key immediately to its **right.** This key may be either **black** or **white.** Eg: the note **F sharp** (written as F♯) is shown on the staff above.

The Note F Sharp (F♯)

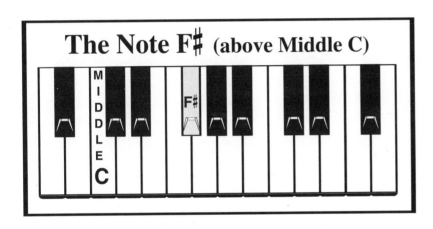

To play the note **F♯**, play the **black** key immediately to the **right** of the F note (white key), as shown on the diagram.

 ## 24. The William Tell Overture

| Suggested Voice : TRUMPET |
| Suggested Rhythm: ROCK |

Most of the notes in this song are played staccato as indicated by the dot placed under or over the note.

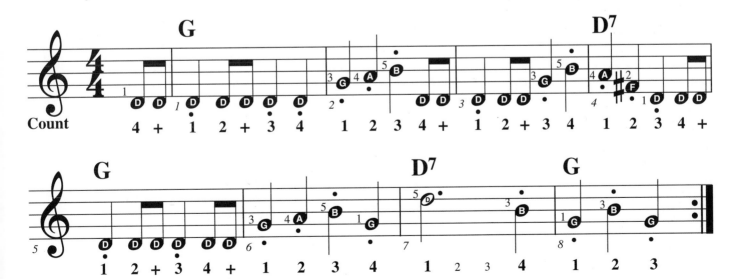

Lesson 7

The Dotted Quarter Note

A dot written after a **quarter note** indicates that you should hold the note for **one and a half** beats. A dotted quarter note is often followed by an eighth note.

Count **1** 2 **+**

Dotted quarter note followed by an eighth note.

25.

Suggested Voice : PIANO

Count   **1**   2   +   **3**   **4**

26. Lullaby

Johannes Brahms

Suggested Voice : PAN FLUTE
Suggested Rhythm: WALTZ

This well known melody written by classical composer **Brahms** makes use of dotted quarter notes in bars 1, 3, 9 and 13.

First and Second Endings

The next song contains **first and second endings**. The **first** time you play through the song, play the first ending, (⌐1.⌐), then go back to the beginning. The **second** time you play through the song, play the second ending (⌐2.⌐) instead of the first.

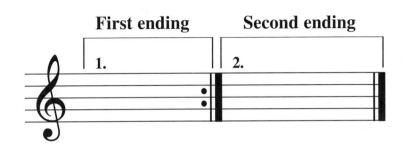

 27. Jingle Bells

| Suggested Voice : XYLOPHONE |
| Suggested Rhythm: RHUMBA |

Jingle Bells is one of the most popular christmas songs. Play to the end of bar 8, then go back to the beginning and play through the song again but play bars 9 and 10 instead of bars 7 and 8.

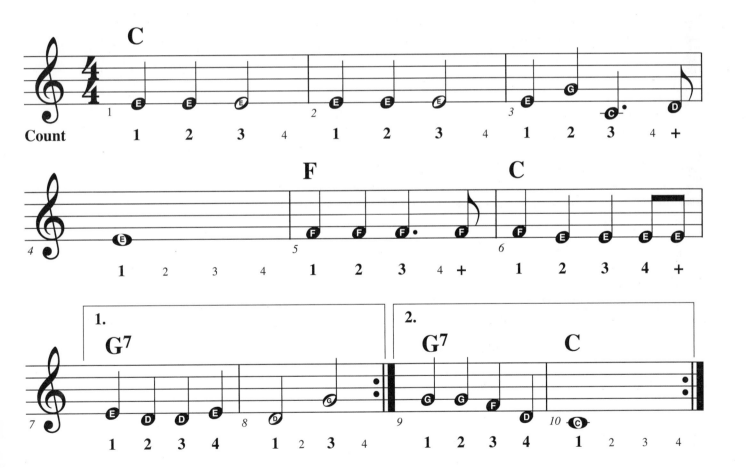

Minor Chords

There are **three** main types of chords: **major**, **seventh** and **minor** chords. You have already learnt some major chords and some seventh chords. The first **minor** chord you will learn is the **D minor** chord. Minor chords are indicated by a small "**m**" written after the chord name, e.g. **Dm**.

The D Minor Chord

Chord Symbol

Type 1 Keyboards
(eg: Yamaha and Technics)
To play a **Dm** chord on this type of keyboard, press the **D** key shown on the diagram with the **thumb** of your left hand, together with the **black** key immediately to its **left,** using your **second** finger.

Type 2 Keyboards
(Casio)
To play a **Dm** chord on this type of keyboard, press the **D** key shown on the diagram with the **second** finger of your left hand, together with the **white** key to its **right,** using your **thumb.**

Type 3 Keyboards
(eg: Roland and Kawai)
To play a **Dm** chord on this type of keyboard, press the **D** key shown on the diagram with the **fifth** finger of your left hand, together with the **third** key to its **right,** using your **third** finger.

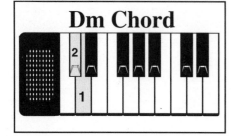

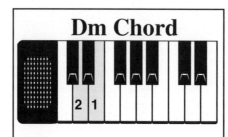

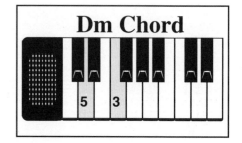

The Common Time Signature

C This symbol is called **common time**. It means exactly the same as $\frac{4}{4}$.

28. Mussi Den

| Suggested Voice : ELECTRIC GUITAR |
| Suggested Rhythm: ROCK |

Mussi Den is a well known song from Germany. The accompaniment contains a **Dm** chord in bar **13**.

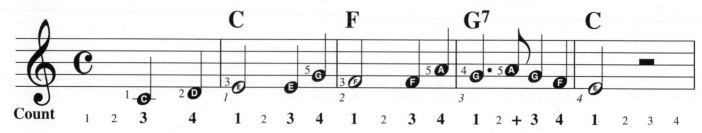

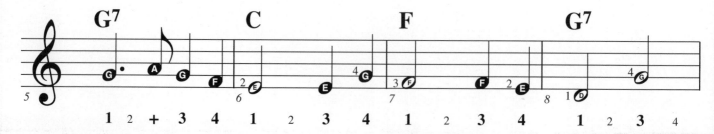

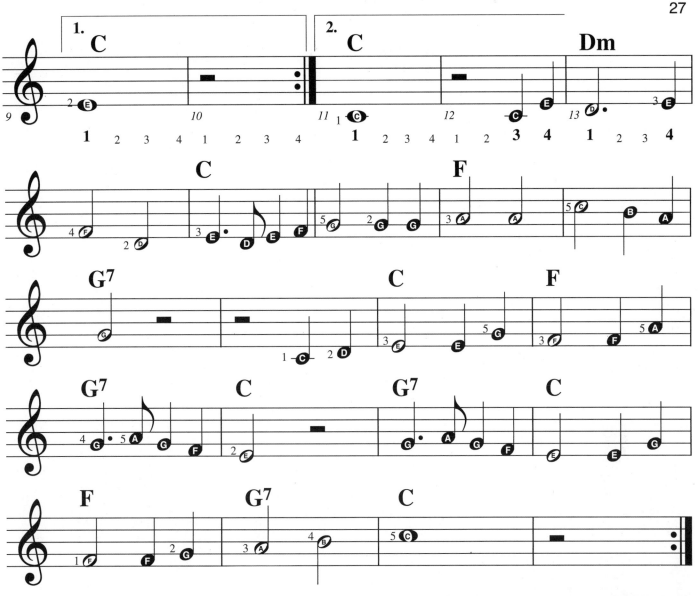

 29. Scarborough Fair

Suggested Voice : 12 STRING GUITAR
Suggested Rhythm: WALTZ

This song is a folk standard. The accompaniment uses the **Dm** chord frequently throughout the song.

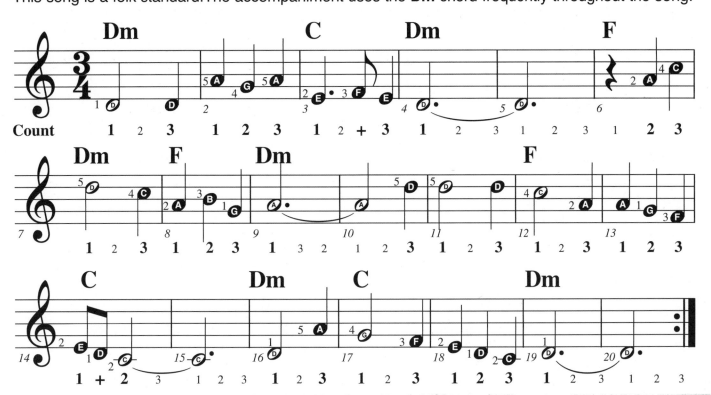

Turnaround Progressions

A **Turnaround** progression is a set pattern of chords that repeats. There are hundreds of well known songs based upon these Turnaround progressions. All these songs contain basically the same chords in the same order. A Turnaround may repeat over any number of bars, usually 2, 4 and 8 bars. However, the **chord sequence** remains the same. Some of the biggest hit records of all time have been based upon a Turnaround progression. Turnarounds always contain at least one **minor** chord. The Turnaround below uses a new chord **E minor** (Em).

Chord Symbol

The E Minor Chord

Em

Type 1 Keyboards
(eg: Yamaha and Technics)

To play an **Em** chord on this type of keyboard, press the **E** key shown on the diagram with the **third** finger of your left hand, together with the **black** key immediately to its **left,** using your **fourth** finger.

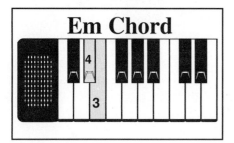

Type 2 Keyboards
(Casio)

To play an **Em** chord on this type of keyboard, press the **E** key shown on the diagram with the **fourth** finger of your left hand, together with the **white** key to its **right,** using your **third** finger.

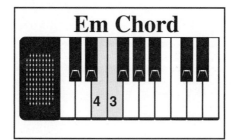

Type 3 Keyboards
(eg: Roland and Kawai)

To play an **Em** chord on this type of keyboard, press the **E** key shown on the diagram with the **fifth** finger of your left hand, together with the **third** key to its **right,** using your **third** finger.

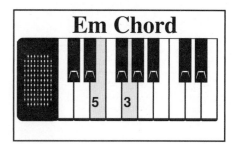

The following Turnaround is in the key of **G** and will probably sound familiar to you.

30.

Suggested Voice : TROMBONE
Suggested Rhythm: ROCK AND ROLL

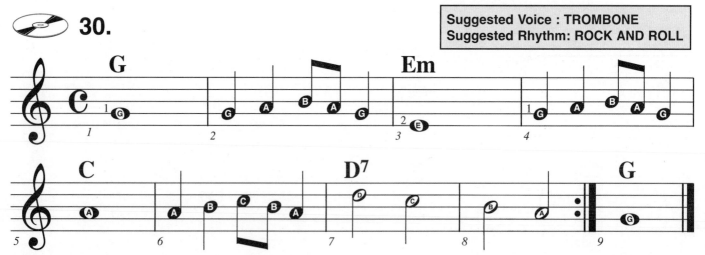

Some songs based on a Turnaround progression are:

Stand by Me - John Lennon
I Will Always Love You - Whitney Housten
Return to Sender - Elvis Presley
All I Have to do is Dream - Everly Brothers
Be My Baby - Ronettes
Everlasting Love - U2

Can't Smile Without You - Barry Manilow
Please Mr Postman - The Beatles
Blue Moon - Various Artists
Tell Me Why - The Beatles
Lets Twist Again - Chubby Checker

The A Minor Chord

Am

Type 1 Keyboards
(eg: Yamaha and Technics)
To play an **Am** chord on this type of keyboard, press the **A** key shown on the diagram with the **third** finger of your left hand, together with the **black** key immediately to its **left,** using your **fourth** finger.

Type 2 Keyboards
(Casio)
To play an **Am** chord on this type of keyboard, press the **A** key shown on the diagram with the **fourth** finger of your left hand, together with the **white** key to its **right,** using your **third** finger.

Type 3 Keyboards
(eg: Roland and Kawai)
To play an **Am** chord on this type of keyboard, press the **A** key shown on the diagram with the **fifth** finger of your left hand, together with the **third** key to its **right,** using your **third** finger.

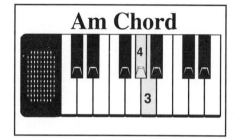

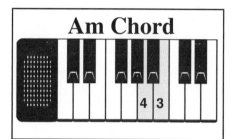

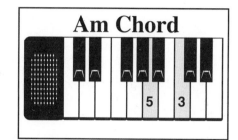

 31. Minuet   J.S. Bach

Suggested Voice : HARPSICHORD
Suggested Rhythm: BEGUINE

The melody of this song was a number one hit record and was based on a minuet by famous classical composer **Bach.** This song introduces the note **B** below middle C in Bars 7 and 15.

32. Morning Has Broken

Suggested Voice : STRINGS
Suggested Rhythm: WALTZ

Morning has Broken uses all the chords you have learnt so far. It also introduces the note **A** below middle C in bar 17.

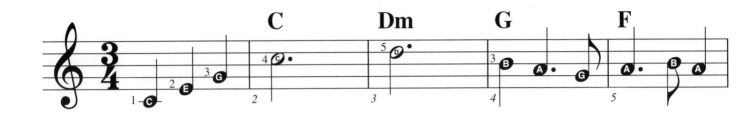

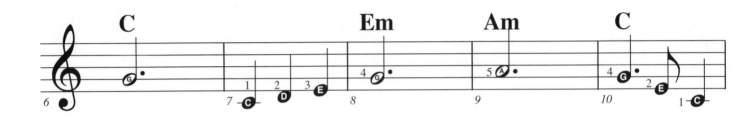

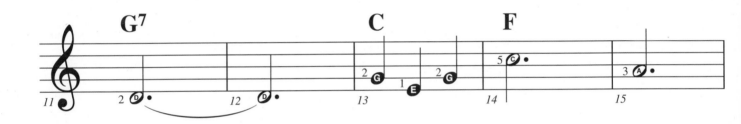

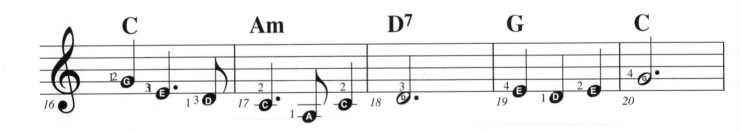

Lesson 8

The G Major Scale

In Lesson 5 the **C Major scale** was introduced. The **G major scale** starts and ends on the note **G**, and contains an **F♯** note instead of an F note. Play the following G major scale and notice that it still has the familiar sound **Do Re Mi Fa So La Ti Do**.

33.

Suggested Voice : PIANO

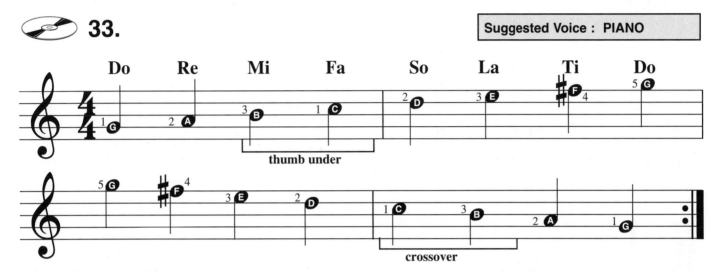

The key of C major was discussed on page 19. Songs that use notes from the **C major scale** are said to be in the **key of C**. Similarly, songs that use notes from the **G major scale** are said to be in the key of **G major**. Songs in the key of G will contain **F sharp** notes.

Key Signatures

Instead of writing a sharp sign before every **F** note on the staff, it is easier to write just one sharp sign after each clef. This means that **all** the F notes on the staff are played as **F♯**, even though there is no sharp sign written before them. This is called a **key signature**.

This is the key signature for the key of **G major**. It has **one sharp sign** after each clef.

The C major scale contains no sharps or flats, therefore the key signature for the key of **C major** contains **no sharps or flats**.

34. I Yi Yi Yi (Cielito Lindo)

Suggested Voice : TRUMPET
Suggested Rhythm: WALTZ

The song **I Yi Yi Yi** is in the key of **G major**. Notice the key signature and play all **F** notes as **F#**. This is one of the most well known songs from Mexico.

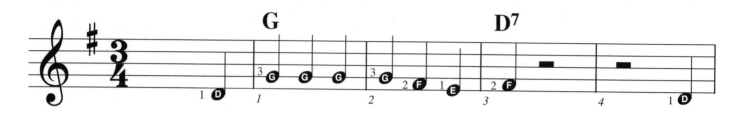

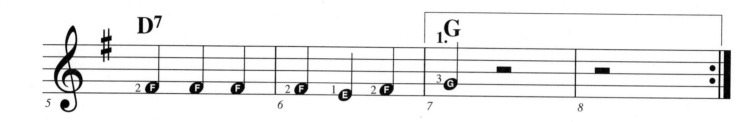

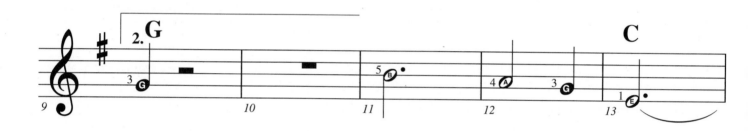

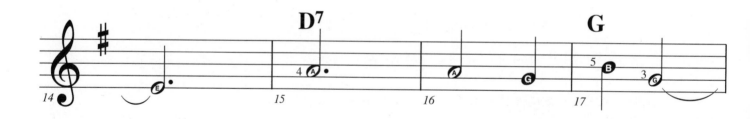

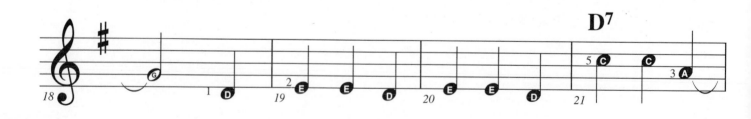

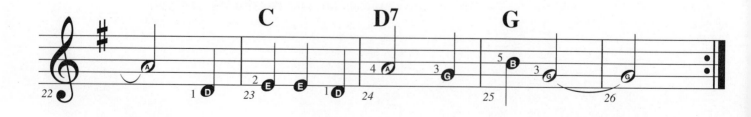

Chopsticks

 ## 35. Chopsticks

Suggested Voice : PIANO

Chopsticks is one of the most well known pieces of music for piano. If your hand is not big enough to stretch the octave in bar 7 you can play the whole song using two hands. This song is in the key of **C major** as indicated by the key signature (i.e. no sharps of flats). Play the melody of Chopsticks without a chord accompaniment.

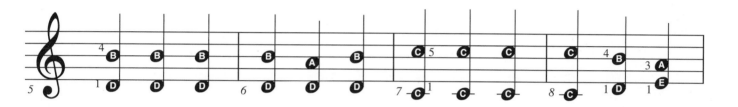

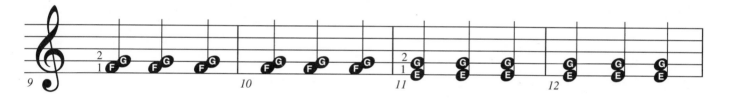

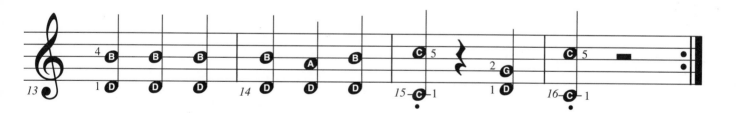

Sloop John B

This song is in the key of **G major**. There is a tie between an eighth note and a quarter note in bar 13. This gives an "off beat" feel called **syncopation**.

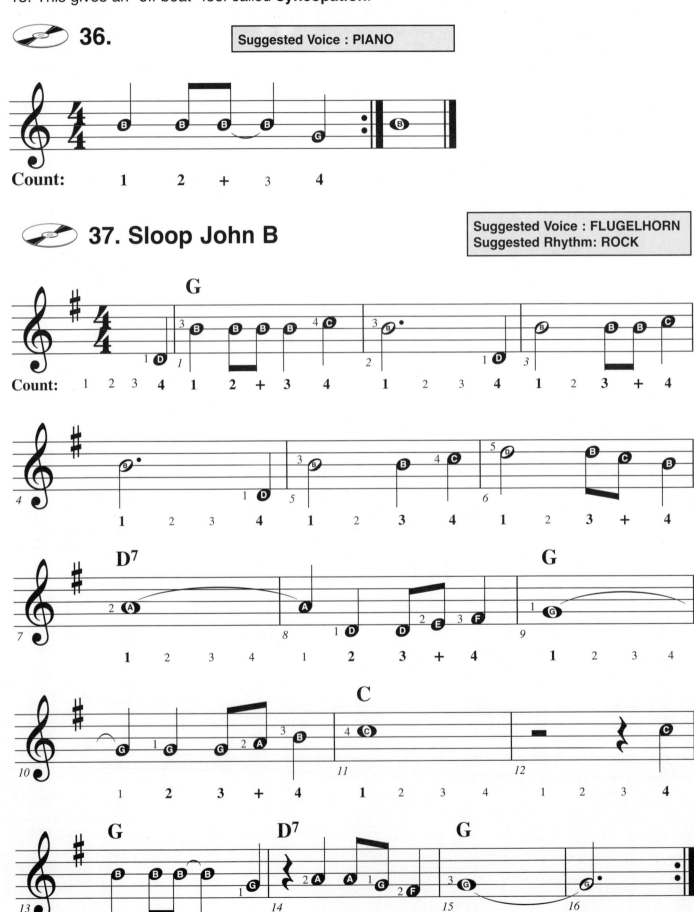

Lesson 9

12 Bar Blues

12 Bar Blues is a pattern of chords which repeats every 12 bars. There are hundreds of well known songs based on this chord progression, i.e., they contain basically the same chords in the same order. 12 bar Blues is commonly used in Rock music and is the basis of Blues music.

Some well known Rock and Roll songs which use this 12 bar chord pattern are:

Original Batman T.V. Theme
Hound Dog - Elvis Presley
Rock Around The Clock - Bill Haley
Roll Over Beethoven - Chuck Berry
Blue Suede Shoes - Elvis Presley
In The Mood - Glen Miller

Shake, Rattle and Roll - Bill Haley
Barbara Ann - The Beach Boys
Johnny B. Goode - Chuck Berry
Dizzy Miss Lizzy - The Beatles
Surfin' U.S.A. - The Beach Boys
Good Golly Miss Molly - Little Richard

 ### 38. 12 Bar Blues in the Key of C Major

The following 12 bar Blues is the key of **C major**, and uses some of the chords you have learned so far. When a song is said to be in the key of C major, it means that the most important chord (and usually the first chord) is the **C** chord.

To finish a 12 Bar Blues, press the **ending** button, (as on the recording), or play one bar of the opening chord (in this case a C chord), and press the **stop** button.

This pattern of chords will probably sound familiar to you.

Suggested Rhythm: ROCK AND ROLL

On the recording there are **two bars** introduction to this 12 bar Blues.

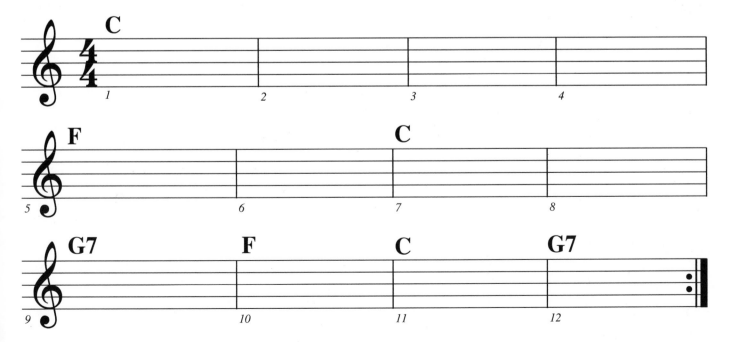

Flat Signs

This is a **flat** sign.

When a flat sign is placed before a note on the staff, it means that you play the key immediately to its **left.** This key may be either black or white. The note **B flat** (written as **B♭**) is a black key. It is shown on the staff above.

The Note B Flat

To play the note **B♭**, play the black key immediately to the left of the **B** note (white note), as shown on the diagram.

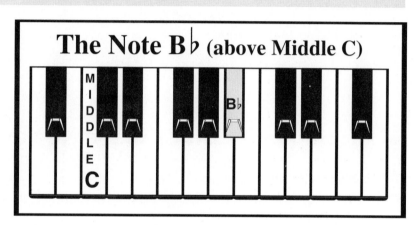

39. 12 Bar Blues in the Key of C Major

This 12 Bar Blues in the key of C makes use of the note **B♭**.

Suggested Voice : ELECTRIC GUITAR
Suggested Rhythm: RHYTHM AND BLUES

The Key of F Major

The **F major scale** starts and ends on the note **F**, and it contains a **B flat** note instead of a B note. Play the F major scale below and listen for the **Do Re Mi Fa So La Ti Do** sound. Songs that use notes from the F major scale are in the **key of F major** and hence contain the note B♭.

 **40.**

Suggested Voice : PIANO

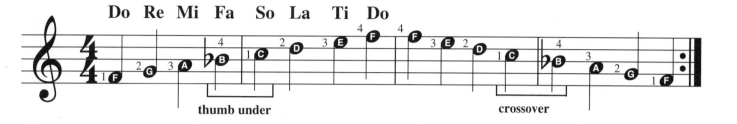

thumb under   crossover

Key Signature of F Major

Instead of writing the flat sign before every B note on the staff, **one** flat sign can be written after each clef. This means that **all** B notes on the staff are played as **B♭**, even though there is no flat sign written before them. This is the key signature for the key of **F major**. There is one flat sign after each clef.

 41. Marianne

Suggested Voice : ELECTRIC PIANO
Suggested Rhythm: HAWAIIAN

This Carribbean folk song is in the key of **F major**.

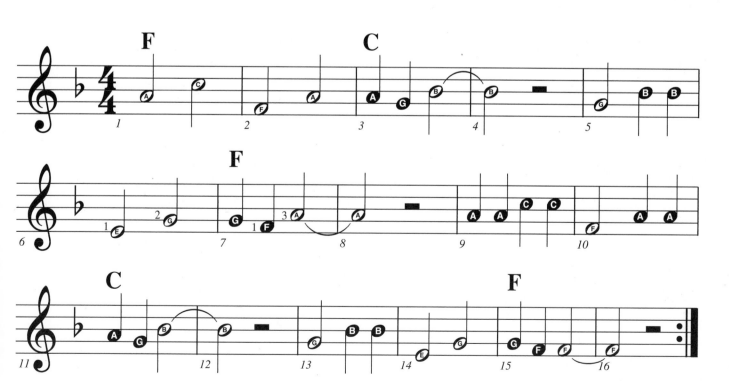

42. Molly Malone

Suggested Voice : REED ORGAN
Suggested Rhythm: WALTZ

The song **Molly Malone** (also called "**Cockles And Mussles**") is a well known traditional Irish song and is written below in the key of **F major**.

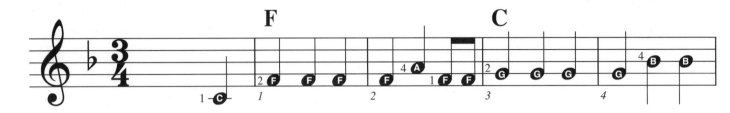

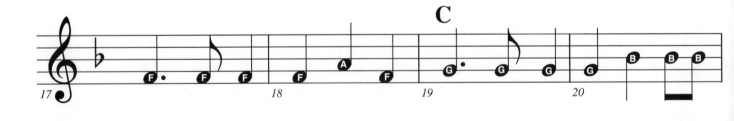

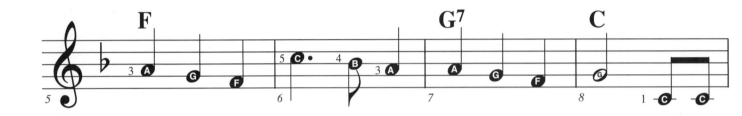

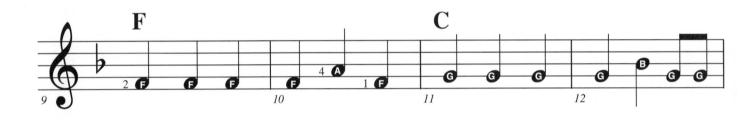

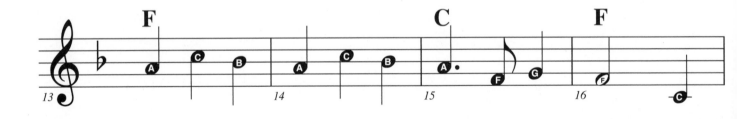

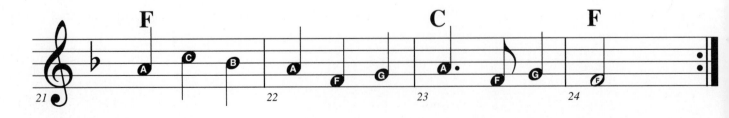

The B Flat Chord

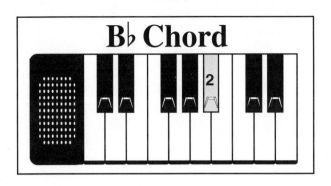

To play the **B♭** chord, touch the **lowest B♭** key with the **second** finger of your left hand, as shown in the diagram.

 ## 43. A Bicycle Built for Two

Suggested Voice : CLARINET
Suggested Rhythm: WALTZ

This song contains a **B♭ chord** and a **B♭ note**. It is in the **key of F major** as indicated by the key signature.

Lesson 10

Left Hand Chords

So far all of the chords you have played have involved only one or two fingers of your left hand. This is because the keyboard is programmed to automatically provide all of the notes of the chord when the correct keys are pressed down. However, chords usually contain at least **three** notes. If you intend to play the piano or become a competent musician on the keyboard you will need to know how to play full chords with your left hand. This means you will need to know how to read **bass clef** as well as treble clef. The bass clef and bass staff are shown below.

Bass Clef

 This symbol is called a **bass clef**.

Bass Staff

A staff with a bass clef written on it is called a **bass staff**.

Notes on the Bass Staff

To remember the notes on the lines of the bass staff, say:
Good **B**oys **D**eserve **F**ruit **A**lways.

To remember the notes in the spaces of the bass staff, say:
All **C**ows **E**at **G**rass.

The Grand Staff

For the melody and accompaniment style of keyboard playing used in this book, the **melody** (played by the right hand) is written on the **treble staff** and the **chords** (played by the left hand) can be written on the **bass staff**. In piano music and most sheet music, the treble and bass staves are bracketed together to create what is known as a **grand staff**. The grand staff is shown below.

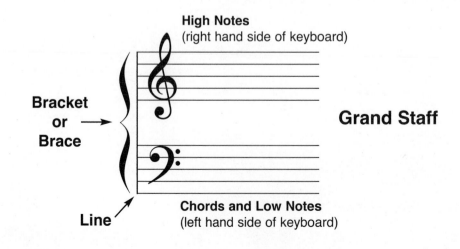

To play fingered chords you will have to select the correct setting on your keyboard. • For **Type 1 Keyboards (eg: Yamaha)**, find the **auto bass chord section** and select the **fingered** position. • For **Type 2 Keyboards (eg: Casio)** find the **Casio-chord section** and select the **fingered** position. • For **Type 3 Keyboards (eg: Roland and Kawai)**, find the **chord intelligence** button and select the **off** position. The first two chords presented here are **C** and **G7**. These chords were introduced as one and two finger chords in lesson 2. They are shown below with the full left hand fingerings. Notice the use of the bass staff to write the notes of the chords. The C note in this chord is **one octave below middle C**.

The **C** chord contains three notes - **C**, **E** and **G**. To play the **C** chord use the **first**, **third** and **fifth** fingers of your left hand, as shown in the **C** chord diagram.

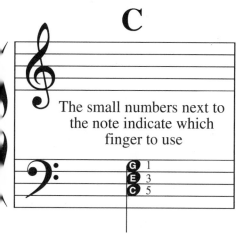

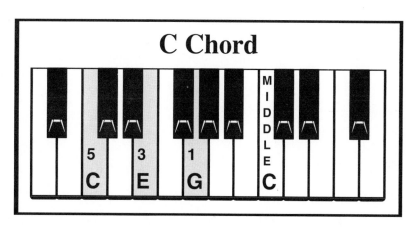

The **G7** chord contains a new note - the **B** next to the C below Middle C. Play the B with the **fifth** finger of your left hand, and use your **first** and **second** fingers to play the G and F notes, as shown in the **G7** chord diagram.

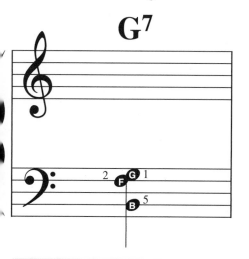

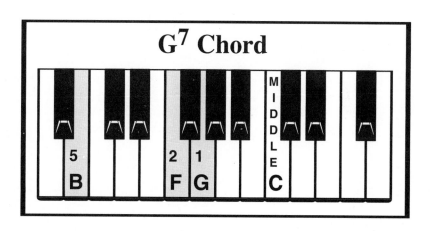

Changing Chords

Practice changing between the **C** and **G7** chords. As both these chords contain the same **G** note, changing between them is quite easy because the **thumb** stays in the same position. It is important to always use the correct fingering when playing notes and chords.

 **44.**

45. Ode to Joy

This song was introduced in lesson 2. It is shown here on the grand staff with the full chord fingerings for **C** and **G7**. Practice the chords separately at first, then play both parts together.

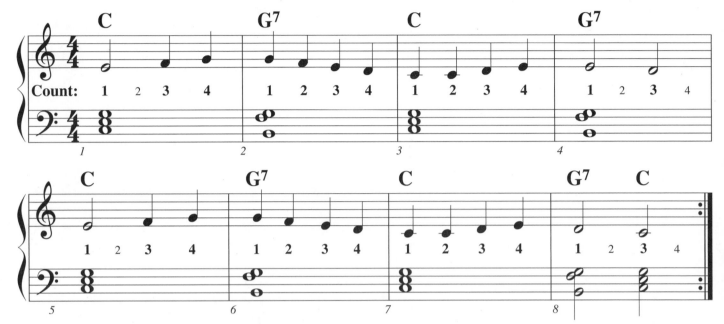

 ## 46. Austrian Waltz

Here is a new version of the **Austrian Waltz** which you learnt in lesson 4. It is in the **key of C major** and uses the chords **C** and **G7**. When you are playing full chords you will need to determine the length of time they sound by the way you play instead of automatically holding the shape down until the next chord change. Notice the use of rests in this song. This means you will need to lift your fingers off the keys with both hands to stop the chord sounding as well as the melody note.

The next chord you will learn to play is the **F** chord. To play the **F** chord, use the **first, second** and **fifth** fingers of your left hand, as shown in the F chord diagram. The **F** chord introduces the note **A** below middle C.

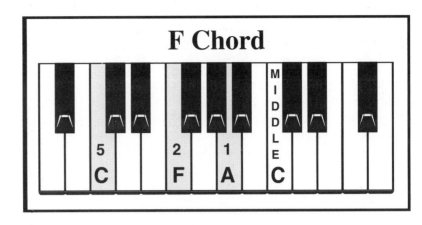

When changing between the **C** and **F** chords keep your **fifth** finger in position as this note is common to both chords. When changing between the **F** and **G7** chords keep your **second** finger in position as this note is common to both chords. Practice changing between **C**, **F** and **G7**.

47. When the Saints Go Marchin' In

When the Saints Go Marchin' In was introduced in lesson 3. Here is a new version which uses full chords in the left hand part. It contains the chords **C**, **F** and **G7**. Once you are comfortable with these chords, go back through the book and play some of the other songs you know using full chords instead of the one and two finger versions.

44

Root Position Chords

There is always more than one way to play any chord on the keyboard. As long as the correct notes are contained within the chord, it is possible to arrange these notes in any order. The different arrangements of the notes are called **inversions**. For a more detailed explanation of inversions, see **10 Easy Lessons for Blues Piano**. The name note of the chord is called the **root note**, eg: the root note of a **C chord** is **C**, the root note of a **G7 chord** is **G**, etc. When the root note is the **lowest** note of the chord shape (fingering), the chord is said to be in **root position**. The C chord shape you learnt earlier in this lesson was in root position. Here are the chords **F** and **G** shown in root position. The **fifth**, **third** and **first** fingers of the left hand are used for both chords.

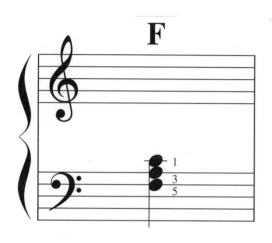

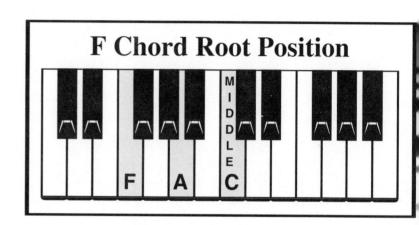

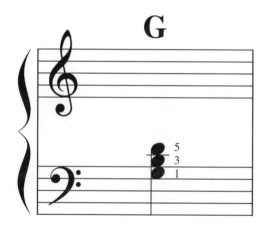

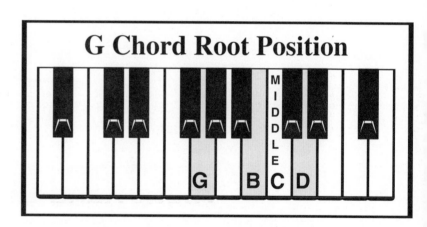

 **48.**

The following example contains the chords **C**, **F** and **G** in root position. Because all of the chords are played with the first, third and fifth fingers of the left hand, a complete shift of position is required each time the chords change. This is easier once you realise that all three chords are the **same chord shape** moved up and down the keyboard. Practice the left hand by itself at first if necessary.

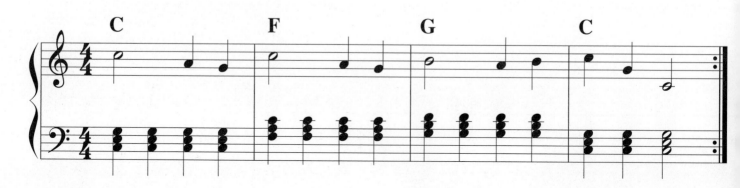

49.

Here is a 12 bar Blues making use of the root postion chords you have just learnt, along with the **G7** chord from earlier in the lesson. The chords are played as eighth notes, which may take some practice before you are comfortable with it, but eighth note left hand parts are common in styles such as Rock, Blues and Funk. The melody played by the right hand is all in one hand position, so all the notes will be right under your fingers. Notice the use of ties to create syncopated rhythms in this example.

Right Hand Chords

Another common technique used in keyboard playing is to play chords with the **right hand** and to play the root note of the chord with the left hand. The easiest way to start learning chords with the right hand is to memorize the chord shapes you already know and move them further up the keyboard. The fingering for each chord will change when you use the right hand, but the **chord shape** remains the same. The example below contains the chords **C**, **F** and **G** in root position played first by the left hand and then the right hand. Both hands use the **first**, **third** and **fifth** fingers to play the chords, but the order is reversed for each hand, ie: left hand – 5, 3, 1, right hand – 1, 3, 5.

50.

46

In the following example the chords **C**, **F** and **G** are played by the right hand while the left hand plays the root notes of the chords. The two hands alternate to create a rocking back and forth effect. This style works well when accompanying a singer or a lead instrument such as a guitar or saxophone.

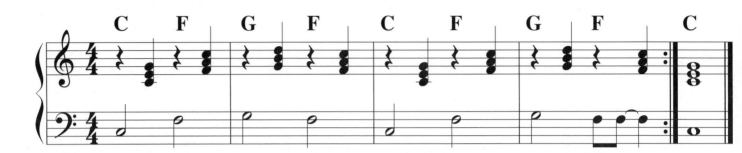

Arpeggios

This 12 bar Blues once again uses the chords **C**, **F** and **G** in root position, but this time they are played **arpeggio** style. An arpeggio is a chord played one note at a time. For more information on arpeggios, see **10 Easy Lessons for Piano**.

Here are two new chord shapes to be played by the left hand. The first is a different version of the **G** chord and the second is **D7**. These chord shapes are important for playing songs in the key of G major. To play this **G** chord, use the **first**, **third** and **fifth** fingers of your left hand, as shown in the **G** chord diagram.

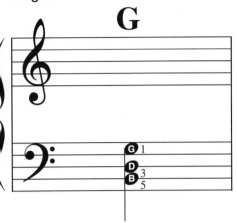
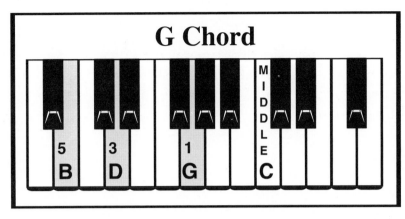

The **D7** chord contains an **F sharp** note which is the black key immediately to the **right** of the F note (white key) below middle C. This **F♯** note is written on the **fourth** line of the bass staff. To play the **D7** chord, use the **first, third** and **fourth** fingers of your left hand as shown in the **D7** chord diagram.

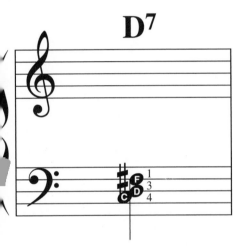
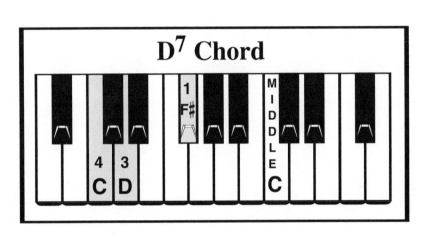

 ## 53. Carnival of Venice

This traditional Italian song makes use of the chords **G** and **D7** shown above. When changing between **G** and **D7**, keep your **third** finger in position as this note is common to both chords. This song also introduces the note **E** above the C one octave above middle C.

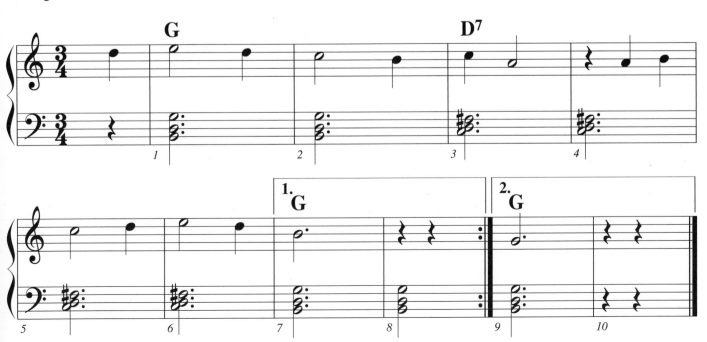

54. 500 Miles

The song **500 Miles** is in the **key of G major** and uses the chords **G** and **D7** along with **C** and **G7**. When changing chords, always look for notes common to both chords. This means you can use the same finger, which will make chord changes easier. You now know enough chord shapes to play hundreds of songs in the keys of **C major** and **G major**. Go back through the book and find other songs to harmonize with these chords and look through the sheet music at your local music store for more songs. For a more in-depth study of chords and accompaniment techniques, see **10 Easy Lessons for Piano**. For more on 12 bar Blues and right hand chords see **10 Easy Lessons for Blues Piano**.

Notes on the Keyboard

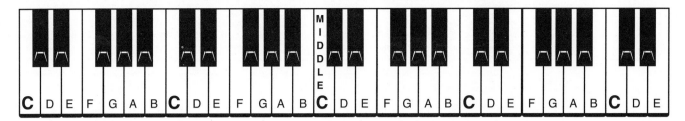

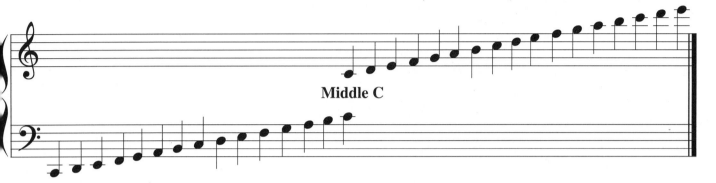

Middle C

Fingered Chord Chart

In this book you are introduced to **major**, **minor** and **seventh** chords. The chord charts on the following pages show three different positions for each of these chord types.
A: The **root position** - This shape has the **root note** (i.e. the note the chord is named after) as the **lowest** note of the chord.
B: The **first and second inversions** contain the **same** notes as the root position but have them in a **different** order.
Other important chord types are **minor seventh (m7)**, **Augmented (+)**, **Diminished (o)**, **Sixth (6)**, **Suspended (Sus)**, **Ninth (9)** etc.

Easy Chord Table

When playing from sheet music and you come across an unfamiliar chord, study the table below to find an easier chord to play. This chord will still sound correct. E.g., when you see a **Cmaj7** symbol, play a **C** chord instead. For a **Cm6**, you can substitute a **Cm** chord, etc.

Chord Written on Sheet Music		Use This Chord
7	- Seventh	**Major**
6	- Sixth	
maj7	- Major Seventh	
sus	- Suspended	
9	- 9th	**Seventh (7)**
11	- Eleventh	
13	- Thirteenth	
m6	- Minor Sixth	**Minor (m)**
m7	- Minor Seventh	
m(maj)7	- Minor Major Seventh	

Major Chord Chart

Chord Name	Notes In Chord	Root Position	First Inversion	Second Inversion
C	C E G			
Db (C#)	Db F Ab			
D	D F# A			
Eb	Eb G Bb			
E	E G# B			
F	F A C			
F# (Gb)	F# A# C#			
G	G B D			
Ab	Ab C Eb			
A	A C# E			
Bb	Bb D F			
B	B D# F#			

Minor Chord Chart

Chord Name	Notes In Chord	Root Position	First Inversion	Second Inversion
Cm	C E♭ G			
C♯m	C♯ E G♯			
Dm	D F A			
E♭m	E♭ G♭ B♭			
Em	E G B			
Fm	F A♭ C			
F♯m	F♯ A C♯			
Gm	G B♭ D			
G♯m	G♯ B D♯			
Am	A C E			
B♭m	B♭ D♭ F			
Bm	B D F♯			

Seventh Chord Chart

Chord Name	Notes In Chord	Root Position	First Inversion (5th omitted)	Second Inversion (3rd omitted)
C7	C E G B♭			
D♭7	D♭ F A♭ C♭			
D7	D F♯ A C			
E♭7	E♭ G B♭ D♭			
E7	E G♯ B D			
F7	F A C E♭			
F♯7 (G♭7)	F♯ A♯ C♯ E			
G7	G B D F			
A♭7	A♭ C E♭ G♭			
A7	A C♯ E G			
B♭7	B♭ D F A♭			
B7	B D♯ F♯ A			